Wisdom TALKS

WE MUST GO BACK TO OUR ROOTS TO WALK INTO OUR FUTURE.

DARLENE BRUCE-SPENCER

TRILOGY
PROFESSIONAL PUBLISHING MEETS POWERFUL PROMOTION
A wholly owned subsidiary of TBN

Wisdom Talks
Trilogy Christian Publishers
A Wholly Owned Subsidiary of Trinity Broadcasting Network
2442 Michelle Drive
Tustin, CA 92780

For information about special discounts for bulk purchases, please contact Trilogy Christian Publishing.
Manufactured in the United States of America
Trilogy Disclaimer: The views and content expressed in this book are those of the author and may not necessarily reflect the views and doctrine of Trilogy Christian Publishing or the Trinity Broadcasting Network.
10 9 8 7 6 5 4 3 2 1
Library of Congress Cataloging-in-Publication Data is available.
ISBN 979-8-89041-184-6
ISBN (ebook) 979-8-89041-185-3

DEDICATION

This book is dedicated to the ones who have inspired me to become the best me. First and always, I am inspired by Yahweh, Father, Son, and Holy Ghost, Elohim, Yeshua, Papa, Our Father, Creator of Heaven and Earth. He promises what He has started He will bring to completion.

I am so grateful to my parents, Edmund and Rhoda Spears, for the life they lived before me as best friends and a united team. Thank you for telling me the prophecies of Yeshua walking amongst us and teaching me to honor Him, to be truthful, and to be responsible in word and deed. Thank you for instilling in me the need to teach these principles and the truths of the Creator, His Son, and the Holy Spirit to the next seven generations. Thank you for demonstrating your love for Yahweh, each other, family, and friends. Thank you for teaching me to be generous and that a smile goes a long way.

I am so thankful for their lives and all the goodness that they showed me. I believe my parents have joined the cloud of witnesses where they continue to pray for family and friends.

To Fred, Jolleen and Ani Webster, Ehrin, Jessica, Quinn and Christian Hunt: each of you have blessed me in thousands of ways. My prayer is that you draw closer to the Creator of all things and find yourself within these pages.

You all have reminded me to be authentically me. "Thank you" will never be enough; Kawanamush, I love you to the moon and back. I appreciate each of you for being the arms, feet, voice, and provision of God in words and deed. So proud of my tribe.

To the Pokanoket Tribe's leadership who have covenanted with Yahweh and Yeshua as our supreme leader. Praise the Lord! They have taught me to be courageous. Oh, how I love you.

Thank you to my pastors Frank and Donna Reedy and my family at Sacred Exchange Fellowship. There are not enough words to express my appreciation of your direction, correction, and protection displayed through the love of our Redeemer. Like Jesus, you all have loved me just as I am while spurring me on to greater things. Special acknowledgement to Julie Chabbot Leo, the illustrator who stepped out of her comfort zone in humility and saw this project through, covering me in so many ways, in love. She would prefer I say nothing of her generosity; I convinced her the world needs to hear these testimonies. She reminds me of the story of the corn husk doll never receiving a face. The reason is, we are all the same and we help each other. I love you all and how we are fitted together.

Dedication

To my gracious employment counselor, Mark Allen, who showed me who I am and the gift I must share. I am ever grateful for your insight, your friendship, and love. I love you back.

To John Roderick and Susan Storti: he is my fratello, my brother, and she, my sister. They are humble, loving, and generous. They both have the gift of tears and giving. We have laughed and cried together; you both have showed me that the hand of God is always very nearby.

I will take these gifts you have deposited and remember the beauty of the feet of those that come in the name of the Lord. I love you.

To the Olerio Family: who I call family, friends, confidants, accountability partners. There is only one word that describes the type of love you have shown me, agape love. I would have to write a novel with the years of you all being there for me and I for you. All we need is love.

All Glory to Yahweh, my Papa, for showing me what Good First may look like in heart, mind, and spirit. Thank you for listening, correcting, directing, and protecting, all the while encouraging me to trust You more and more. Surrendering to Your perfect love I see Your hand molding me into purpose.

Thank You, Yeshua, my Husband. I am preparing

for Your return; Your warrior bride patiently awaits her King, staying alert, prepared in and out of season as I am quickened by the Holy Spirit.

Holy Spirit (Aw sha bar le tar nay), thank You for activating angels and being ever beside me, filling me with joy and fire. Breathe on me again.

FOREWORD

From the author: though this book is written as fiction, much of it is made up of true stories from my childhood. I was told Yeshua walked with us here on Turtle Island, the Americas as we know them now. He gave us the Holy Spirit and told of others that would bring the Word. He gave us provision of the Three Sisters and in the provision are parables denoting the nature of our Heavenly Father, Yahweh, Yeshua, and Holy Spirit.

The Bible was translated into the Algonquin language for the praying Indians of the Pokanoket Tribe and other Northeastern woodland tribes at the birth of this nation. He is the God of every tribe and every nation. To all who believe in Him, He gave the right to be a child of God.

All about Yahweh is truth. He loves us, provides for us, fights our every battle, and is victorious every time. He visited us, and when He left, He left us the Holy Spirit to guide us and comfort us. He is to return one day, and all will look up and see Him return from the sky. He has prepared work and a place for those who know Him. His desire is that none be lost. To know Him is to love Him, for Yahweh is love.

If you want to know Him, if you are not sure you will go to heaven, ask Him to reveal Himself to you. He died for a fallen world; acknowledge that in yourself. He became victorious over death so all may have life eternal in heaven with Him. Ask Him to come and sup with you and teach you His ways, to live life in fullness.

To understand this better, read the Gospel of John in the Bible. Ask a friend who you are sure knows, loves, and follows Jesus. They are the peculiar ones. They love instead of hate, forgive what others call unforgiveable, and believe and see the impossible happen in their lives.

Meanwhile, I am praying for you. Prayer reaches the place where time and space are unmeasurable. Aquene (peace be with you). Let peace guide you. Kwannamush (I love you).

Table of Contents

Wisdom Talks

Chapter 1:
LEGACY

The day is near its end; the sun is disappearing beyond the horizon. The sky is painted in bright yellow, red, orange, and purple. It is a spring evening, and the families of the Pokanoket Tribe are gathered at the Community Center, an oblong concrete building made to look as a traditional longhouse would be made, from cedar and bark. The lights are shaped like the torches that were used years ago, made from pine sticks tied in knots.

The Pokanoket are an Eastern Woodland Indigenous people consisting of sixty tribes, bands, and clans. They are the tribe of first contact with the European colonists, helping them to survive their first winters and sharing the first Thanksgiving. The Pokanoket people believe and live by a fundamental rule: the stronger shall care for the weaker.

The entire Pokanoket Tribe is gathering in the Great Room this evening to hear the prophecies of Clan Mother Ukquonokquon Ayeateanen (Rainbow Warrior), who lived many, many years ago. I will tell the story of when she and her sisters met with Yahweh's son Yeshua.

Every spring the prophecies are told at the time of the Strawberry Thanksgiving, the time the Pokanoket Tribe celebrates forgiveness.

At the Strawberry Thanksgiving, the story of a brother and sister who quarreled is told. The boy was so angry that he left home and went to the west and the girl left home and went to the east. After a while they both felt sorry for arguing with each other, for prior to arguing they did everything together. The boy asked Yahweh to forgive him for arguing with his sister. The girl also asked Yahweh to forgive her for arguing with her brother. She asked Yahweh for something special to bring to her brother as a peace offering. Yahweh told her to look down; there at her feet were wild strawberries all around. She tasted one; it was so sweet. She gathered a basket full and brought them to her brother. When she met her brother, she asked him to take the strawberries as a symbol of forgiveness. The boy accepted her gesture of forgiveness. We remember the power of forgiveness each spring when the strawberries are ripe. It is thought to be odd not to ask for forgiveness or not to accept an apology when offence has happened.

This practice keeps unity amongst the community.

Telling stories and sharing traditions are practiced at various times in the Pokanoket Nation. Each spring in the Pokanoket community we tell the Strawberry Thanksgiving story and the story of Ukquonoquon Ayeateanen (Rainbow Warrior). We teach each generation that they are to teach the next seven generations the stories, wisdom, and traditions.

We have had our Strawberry Thanksgiving. All are at peace with each other. Tonight, the story of Yeshua walking amongst the Pokanoket will be told.

The Great Room is large enough to hold 500 people sitting comfortably on fur covered benches. The benches are made in the traditional way, with no backs. The room is lined three benches deep around the perimeters of the oblong structure. The benches are wide enough to recline if one may need mattituck (a place to rest). Many come with blankets to cover those who may fall asleep. This is done to show honor, caring, and love.

The adults are seated shoulder to shoulder and there is very soft chatter as members sit and greet one another. Closeness in all aspects of life with the Pokanoket is common and beautiful. The atmosphere is peaceful and respectful as space is made for elders or those with special needs. The slow pace of assembling continues as members greet and find their clans.

There are five clans; they are wolf, deer, bear, snipe, and turtle. The wolf clan members are leaders, deer are providers, bear have knowledge of medicine, snipe are builders and turtle members know the history.

There is enough room between the rows for young children to sit at their parents' feet. The children are encouraged to play quietly with shells or corn husk dolls, or to make traditional tools. Some are doing elaborate bead work or are working on regalia (the traditional clothing made of deer hide) as the stories are being told. The Pokanoket waste nothing, not even time.

There is an understanding that the children will hear the stories of the prophecies and traditions throughout their lives and may one day become a storyteller.

In the center of the Great Room there is a large, round fireplace; the flue of the fireplace reaches the ceiling. There is ash that originates from previous fires burning in the community fire, representing bringing forth goodness from the previous gathering. A mild aroma of burning oak is in the air; also there are the scents of cedar, sage and sweet grass as there is smudging at the entrance. Smudging is done by burning the cedar, sage and sweetgrass in a large seashell. The smoke is fanned over the front and back of each person with a fan made of feathers as they pray for deliverance from any negative spirits. No one will enter the Great Room without smudging first. This is done prior to every gathering. We will pray that all have good intentions; we pray away any negative spirit that would hinder the meeting from going in a good way. The elements are to represent prayer rising to the Creator and that they are a sweet aroma to His nostrils. Tonight, there is a small flame that has created a soothing golden glow to the room. No one really knows when the first fire was started. The fire is eternal.

The Pokanoket community is here this cool spring evening to hear me tell the prophecies of Yeshua, Yahweh's son, visiting Rainbow Warrior, her sisters, and the Pokanoket Tribe.

I am Kepenum Nepauzshad (Harvest Moon). I am 33 years old, and I am the granddaughter twelve times over of Ukquonokquon Ayeateanen (Rainbow Warrior), one of the Wolf Clan Grandmothers of the Pokanoket Tribe. Being a clan mother is a humbling service. It is both a blessing and a burden.

I have been fasting, praying, and listening to Yahweh. He will speak to the people through me ,for He is in me, and I have surrendered to His will.

I am told I resemble my great grandmother twelve times over, Rainbow Warrior, in stature and character. I am average height and weight for our people. My arms and legs are strong for harvesting and walking up great inclines. My eyes are the darkest of brown, with a ring of deep blue around the parameter of my pupils. My skin is smooth and tawny. My hair is to my waist and amber in color, not like most Pokanoket who have dark brown or black hair. It is said that this amber hair color is a gift from Creator, a sign that shows being set apart.

Rainbow Warrior and I have been described as physically similar. I am also told we are similar in character, both putting our relationship with Yahweh above all else and having a great love for serving our people.

From a young age the elders recognized my gifts. I learned to tell our stories and prophecies by listening to and watching my great-grandmother, grandmother, and mother. Now I will tell the story of Rainbow Warrior meeting Creator Yahweh's son Yeshua, not only in spirit but also face to face.

I have learned to capture my audience's attention through watching, listening to, and emulating my mother's, grandmother's, and great-grandmother's graceful movements and the use of inflection in my voice. They taught me to set myself aside for fasting and prayer days prior to telling the stories. When they told the stories, every eye and ear was fixed on them. All the children would remain quiet; babies never cried. The peace confirmed that Yahweh was present to meet everyone's need.

Chapter 2:

You Take Me to a Place Called Beautiful

I, Harvest Moon, take my position in the center of the room. I listen to the Great Spirit, and I will repeat what He says. I am wearing my traditional deerskin regalia, with leggings and moccasins. My skin is flawless, smooth, and tawny, showing golden undertones in the dim light of the fire. I am to represent to my nation resilience and modesty, a tradition passed down by example.

My stance shows both strength and grace. Gracefully I move; I use inflection in my voice at times of joy, fear, or tenderness. The gift of storytelling given by Yahweh to serve the people will capture all eyes and ears.

I will not need to raise my voice to be heard in the Great Room; the room was made acoustically friendly. I will begin to speak as I listen to Creator speak to me of the story of Ukquonokquon Ayeateanen (Rainbow Warrior). This story took place in the time before the arrival of the Europeans. Harvest Moon looks from the left to the right of the community room. She smiles and says, “I will begin the story of Yeshua visiting our community years ago in the time of my Great-Grandmother twelve times over Ukquonokquon Ayeateanin, Rainbow Warrior.”

****

Rainbow Warrior woke before dawn as she did every day. Her first thoughts were verbalized: “Thank You, Yahweh, Creator of all things, for another day to walk this earth on these lands, to do Your will and to give You praise and thanksgiving.”

Rainbow Warrior has lived forty-nine seasons; her skin was still smooth, taut, and tawny. It glowed in beautiful gold tones in the light of the smoldering fire. Her eyes were the darkest brown with a ring of blue around the perimeter of her pupils.

She rose slowly, not to disturb Wunne Neggone (Good First,) her husband whose name is so fitting. Even in the low light of the longhouse Good First looks handsome, his long, masculine body silhouetted under a mass of deer hide. He has lived forty-three seasons; his hair was pure white and had been pure white since his thirteenth season. It was braided in two braids that rested on his chest. His slow, rhythmic breathing assured Rainbow Warrior that once again she was able to come out from his embrace without waking her husband.

The differences in the seasons they have lived have never affected their friendship or love. Rainbow Warrior thought Good First would be up and moving before she returned from her time alone with Yahweh at their sacred mound Potumtuk, the highest point of Wunne Sowams.

Wunne Sowams means "a beautiful Southern place). Sowams is the place where the governing body of the Pokanoket Tribe met. It was a place of peace and protection. Potumtuk was the highest elevation of Sowams; it is where Rainbow Warrior went to meet Yahweh.

She had prepared the night before for a quick departure, leaving dried fish, strawberries, and water for her family's morning meal by the fire. She saw that the other living areas where her daughters, son-in-laws, and grandchildren live showed no signs of anyone awake. She moved quietly and gracefully about the longhouse to make her way to the opening.

She thought, *I need only to cover with a shawl this spring morning.* Before going to bed the evening prior, she left her shawl along with her prayer elements (cedar, sage, sweetgrass, a large quohog shell, and flint for lighting her prayer elements) near the opening of their longhouse.

Rainbow Warrior and Good First together built this longhouse before their children were born. Their longhouse had kept their family safe and warm for twenty full seasons. Rainbow Warrior and Good First worked well together, making this sturdy home. They worked well together in all life matters, for the two became one under Yahweh's' blessings.

Rainbow Warrior saw that the fire in the center had plenty of embers to keep her family warm for several hours or until her second grandchild, Sunshine and Tethers Close's son, Nootau Pomushaun (Fire Walker), a fire keeper in training, awakened. This ability to keep the fire was knitted into his being. The firekeepers could maintain a fire in any weather.

Sunshine and Tethers Close have a second son, One Who Makes All Laugh. I will tell you more about him later in the story. What is of importance is, since the beginning of time Yahweh has gifted each person with gifts that are given for the betterment of all.

She thanked Yahweh for providing the material to shelter her and her family as she moved towards the longhouse's opening where she grabbed her sacred elements along with her shawl.

She and Good First intended to share their dwelling with any children they were given. Not knowing how many children Creator would bless them with, they built their longhouse large enough to house fifteen to twenty people.

Creator blessed them with two daughters, Fawn, their older, and Sunshine, the younger. Their daughters grew up in this longhouse. Now their daughters, their husbands, and children lived in this sturdy longhouse she and Good First built. Three generations fit together nicely there. They also built an atmosphere of peace, love, and respect for each other, and above all, love for Yahweh, their Creator.

Fawn and her husband, Smiling Wind, gave birth to their first grandchild, a girl. This was Ukquonokquon Nepe'unk (Rainbow Fern), the oldest of the grandchildren. Rainbow Fern had seen ten seasons and was gifted, as Rainbow Warrior was, with a special ear to hear Yahweh's voice. She also had amber hair, a sign that set her apart.

Before Rainbow Warrior left, she scanned the longhouse; she believed all were asleep. Rainbow Warrior prayed in a whisper, "Yahweh, watch over my family and my entire nation today; teach us all Your ways. Teach us to become one with You."

Rainbow Warrior heard the small voice of her granddaughter Rainbow Fern, standing behind her. "A'ho, I agree, Grandmother." They smiled at each other as Rainbow Warrior exited the longhouse. She thought this was a good sign; already a prayer of agreement this morning.

The sky was the darkest blue; the night had not yet transitioned to daylight. The moon was full, glowing in brilliant white. The endless number of twinkling white stars were spread across the deep blue sky. She walked past the forty or more large longhouses, fires, canoes, sleeping dogs, and headed northeast to the path that leads to Potumtuk, the high peak of Sowams.

Her village was simply called Wellnomuck, (Home). Wellnomuck was formed of many large longhouses that housed families and extended families. Many Pokanoket families as large as four generations lived together comfortably in one longhouse. Mothers, fathers, aunts, uncles, and cousins may share one dwelling. There were other areas that were used to smoke deer, turkey, and other game meats or to store herbs, medicines and supplies needed for all to share. The smell of smoke coming from each longhouse permeated the air, filling her nostrils with the smell of home.

The sound of running water was a constant melody at Wellnomuck; waters flow down from the mountains into the river. The clear, fresh water flowed just west of Rainbow Warrior's dwelling. It is where water was drawn daily for drinking and bathing. It is where the youngsters fish, the men clean game, the women wash everything from food to children. The water is removed from the river for use to keep the integrity of the rivers maintained. The Pokanoket understand that the health of the land, air, and the water is their responsibility.

Stewardship of Yahweh's provision is taught from one generation to the next. The rivers and ocean are places of life, death, and great mystery. They are to be respected and maintained. Honor begets honor with all Yahweh's creation.

The glow of the fire outside of the meeting place, the largest longhouse in Wellnomuck, was the last visual Rainbow Warrior would see as she continued her journey to Putumtuk. It is where the Pokanoket gather to socialize, celebrate each moon's thanksgiving, and discuss matters of importance. She will speak to her people outside the community meeting longhouse at the great fire after returning from speaking with Yahweh.

Chapter 3:

FOLLOW ME

Rainbow Warrior would be the only one holding the talking stick today at the meeting place. The talking stick is given to a speaker; when one is holding the talking stick no other will interrupt their speech. Those listening are encouraged to listen for understanding.

The elders at the last moon's meeting decided that only Rainbow Warrior would be holding the talking stick today. It is a great honor and a great burden to speak to Yahweh and to bring His message back to the Pokanoket people.

Rainbow Warrior was born with an ear sensitive to hearing Yahweh's voice. She heard Yahweh call her name many times in her life. "Rainbow Warrior," He would say, "Follow Me." Her answer always the same. "Where You lead me, I will follow, Yahweh."

She continued walking the path leading up to Potumtuk. The dew glistened on the ground in the light of the moon; the fog hanging low in the air looked like low wispy clouds. The smell in the air changed from burning wood to the sweet smell of pine trees.

Rainbow Warrior started to feel the incline in her thighs as she made her way to the crest of Wunne Sowams, Potumtuk. She continued to thank Yahweh for the beauty that is in the sky and on the earth and in the land. She ignored the aches in her thighs and pushed on. She knew that her body would adjust and was thankful that she was still able to push through.

Chapter 4:

Creator, I'm Here

Though Rainbow Warrior had seen forty-nine full seasons, she stands tall and has strong arms, legs, and a strong heart to walk the incline to the crest of Sowam, Potumtuk. She knew that the mild ache in her thighs was building strength and keeping her strong. In her prayer she thanked Yahweh for keeping her mind, body, and spirit strong.

Rainbow Warrior had a look of anticipation as she came to the spot Yahweh had drawn her to since she was a child, an area circled with large stones to the South, North, East, and West. She knew today would be a special time with Yahweh. She felt it in her soul.

Entering the circle from the East, the ocean at her back, the smell of salt in the air fresh and pungent, she walked one full time around the encircled area. Walking to the middle of the circle, she got on her knees facing North, where she will speak to Yahweh.

She removed the large shell, flint, sweetgrass, sage, and cedar from her bag. Rainbow Warrior easily lit the combination of sage, sweetgrass and cedar in her shell with one strike of flint to flint. She softly blew on the embers. The sage, sweetgrass, and cedar dispersed the pleasant aroma of the rising smoke. The aroma of her prayer elements now filled the air. The smoke rose from the shell and Rainbow Warrior sang, "Yahweh, Yah Yah wey Yah Yahweh YahYah wey Yahweh Yah Yah wey Yah Yahweh Yah.

"May my prayer be a sweet aroma to You as the sage, sweetgrass and cedar are to me. I come to You asking You to forgive me for anything that I have done with a bad spirit. Please reveal these things to me, show me and give me Your good spirit to do what is right and pleasing to You. Yahweh, use me as You will. I will be obedient; I will say and do what You ask. No more, no less. I will not speak before hearing You and I will not hesitate to say or do what You ask of me."

Rainbow Warrior decided she would not leave this time she had set apart for Yahweh until Yahweh spoke to her.

Chapter 4: Creator, I'm Here

Chapter 5:

CREATOR, HEAR OUR CRY

Rainbow Warrior continued to pray and listen to Yahweh as the sun came up. The birds began singing their morning songs. The morning breezes accompanied the tall grass and the leaves as all creation came into their morning songs, dances, praises, and thanksgivings to Yahweh. All creation, young and old, was awakening to the new day.

The sun as it lifted from the horizon was fiery red, orange, and yellow. As the sun continued to rise above the horizon it lost the red and orange hues and transitioned to variants of yellow. White clouds began to appear, scattered across an ocean of light blue sky.

Rainbow Warrior continued her prayers, praising, asking for forgiveness, asking for Yahweh's Good Spirit to work through her. She spent much time bringing the needs of all her relations, her tribe, the earth, the air, all the waters, all other peoples and all creatures of the earth before Yahweh. She asked for protection, direction, and correction for all peoples, starting with herself.

Rainbow Warrior sat with her legs folded beneath her; at times she leaned forward, her hands on the ground. On all four limbs she rhythmically rocked and continued to pray. Her spirit made way for the presence of the Spirit of Yahweh. Rainbow Warrior was moved to raise her hands to the sky in adoration of Yahweh. She spent time quietly listening until Yahweh spoke to her spirit. In past times of prayer tears have fallen; other times there is great laughter, but every time there is honor, gratefulness, and beauty. Today Rainbow Warrior was blessed with great clarity in hearing the voice of Yahweh.

Chapter 6:

I Need to Hear Your Voice

The sun was near vertical and warmed Rainbow Warrior's face and shoulders. She deeply breathed in and out. The presence of Yahweh was as tangible as the aroma of cedar, sweetgrass and sage floating on the breeze. Yahweh beckoned Rainbow Warrior to enter "The Most Holy Place." She allowed her mind, body, and soul to come in alignment with the frequency of the Creator of all things. She felt perfect love and peace.

Her tawny skin glowed in the morning sunlight; it glowed with golden tones and her amber hair showed many hues of red, gold, and brown. Everything about Rainbow Warrior's appearance was enhanced in the presence of Yahweh. In these times, in the presence of Yahweh, Rainbow Warrior felt completely whole and at peace.

"Yes, Yahweh, I will speak to the next seven generations of Your wisdom. Thank You that You help us all to do well. Yes, I will do all which I know pleases You. Yes, I am willing to do all You ask of me, Yahweh. Yes, I understand that it may be hard at times; yes, I know You will be there with me always and I need not fear anything or anyone. Thank You, oh Great Mystery, Yahweh, who provides all for Your people in body, mind, and spirit. You alone provide for all creation."

Rainbow Warrior would not leave her post until she heard Yahweh release her to return to Wellnomuk. Whether she sought Yahweh for hours or days, Rainbow Warrior would not leave this place until she heard Yahweh say, "Return home." And when she heard Yahweh say to her that morning, "Return home," Rainbow Warrior did not hesitate. Immediately she got up and gathered her things to go back to Wellnomuck. She has learned that immediate obedience is so important; everything in Yahweh's time.

She walked slower down the mountain back to Wellnomuck, enjoying the freshness of the air, the warmth of the sun and the sounds of creation awakening. She also pondered every word spoken to her by Yahweh this morning.

Nearing the village, she met the sounds and sights of the people of her tribe awakening. The sounds of the village awakening were pleasant in her ears; naturally, she smiled. She saw her own grandchildren doing their morning chores. Granddaughter Ukquonokquon Nepe'unk (Rainbow Fern) was fetching water, grandson Nootau Pomushaen (Fire Walker, who had seen nine seasons, was gathering wood for the fires. Howan Keesuck Wame Ahanu (One Who Makes All Laugh) who was in his sixth season was doing just that, making everyone laugh as he posed, danced, and swirled in ever quickening circles.

She thought, *This is good medicine this morning; all are moving as one for the good of all.* Rainbow Warrior continued to smile; she knew Yahweh was pleased.

Rainbow Warrior walked to the village fire where all would gather to hear the wisdom that she had received from Yahweh. That was her position as Wolf Clan Grandmother; the position was given to her by the elders, the position she was given before she was conceived by her parents, the position given by her Creator, Yahweh. She was to teach the good way to live and encourage all to also teach the next seven generations. She was to be transparent in her frailty so others would be also. There is no room for pride when standing before Yahweh.

The Fire Keeper (Walks Well), has kept the fire burning night and day, rain or shine. He had mastered the art of keeping the sacred fire going. He was mentoring her grandson, Fire Walker, to take his place when the time came.

Good First came out of the longhouse and met Rainbow Warrior at the great fire. He was taller than most of the Pokanoket men; though a man of only forty-three seasons, his hair was completely white. His shoulders were wide, his waist narrow, the formation of firm muscles visible under his regalia. The elders said his hair was white because he had the purest of thoughts.

With a gentle touch and warm dark brown eyes, he came close and embraced Rainbow Warrior. He put his forehead to hers and they looked deeply into one another's eyes. "You are glowing like the sun, my love. Kawannamush (I love you). Creator Yahweh has given you a good word for our people."

"I love you, husband. Yes, Yahweh has spoken to me a good word; He has given you a dream during the night?" she inquired.

"Later we will speak of this; you have to address the people with the good word of Yahweh," he said and smiled. "Your provision for breakfast was very good; we all have eaten and will be joining the rest of the people when you sing the gathering together song."

"Very soon, husband, I will sing." he reaches into her bag and pulled out her hand drum. She neared the fire to warm herself and her drum.

"I will let the others know you will be starting soon

and to be ready," Good First said. He kissed her forehead and squeezed her waist. He has always touched her so tenderly and passionately.

Good First walked away to gather the rest of their family, his stride showing both strength and humility. Rainbow Warrior thought he was as handsome and kind today as when they first met many, many moons earlier.

She had seen eighteen full seasons when she and Good First met. She would often go alone foresting for berries, mushrooms, herbs, and black walnuts. But this early spring morning twenty years ago Rainbow Warrior was not alone. This morning Rainbow Warrior found herself face to face with a black bear. The bear was about fifteen feet tall and was looking right at her from forty feet away. The bear had smelled Rainbow Warrior foresting and was tracking her. The bear's eyes were now fixed on Rainbow Warrior. It stood on its hind legs and roared with such a loud roar that Rainbow Warrior froze, her eyes also fixed on the bear.

She attempted to scream. Rainbow Warrior opened her mouth, but no sound came out. The bear took three leaps towards her and fell with a loud thud to the ground.

Ten feet behind where the bear had fallen stood Good First. Her eyes met with the eyes of this tall handsome young Nipmuc brave, his face so young yet his hair completely white.

Good First had shot three arrows into the lungs of that huge black bear. He had been tracking that bear since early morning. He had no idea he would be saving someone's life by killing the bear. This bear kill would feed and clothe many; also this kill introduced him to his future wife, Rainbow Warrior.

Good First looked at the bear lying dead; his eyes returned to Rainbow Warrior's eyes. He smiled. They both felt an imparting of excitement in their hearts as they looked into each other's eyes.

Good First approached Rainbow Warrior; she was still holding her basket of berries and herbs. Rainbow Warrior was now aware that she was shaking.

Though she knew the language of Nipmuc, she could not speak, for the fear of the bear had not yet left her. Rainbow Warrior attempted to speak but she still was not able to make a sound. Good First sensed the fear in Rainbow Warrior; he quickly approached her, putting his right hand around her waist and his left hand around her neck. He drew Rainbow Warrior into his chest where she finally released her fear. Rainbow Warrior wrapped her arms around him and held Good First so tightly, as if she were holding on for her life. Time seemed to stop there in their first embrace.

Good First was the first to speak. "Are you hurt?" he asked, looking down into Rainbow Warrior's eyes.

"No, I am not hurt; oh, thank you, how did you..." Rainbow Warrior could not finish her sentence. When she investigated the face of this young white-haired brave, she felt safe.

Good First told her his name, that he was Nipmuc, and that he had been tracking that bear since early morning. Rainbow Warrior told Good First her name, that she was Pokanoket, and that she did not realize the bear was there.

Though the two tribes kept distant, there was a good relationship and respect for each other with no history of fighting. They felt comfortable interacting with each other. It was not spoken that day, but later they both said that as this meeting happened there was a sweet smell in the air of pine and honey, good medicine, a good sign.

Good First and Rainbow Warrior worked together to skin and piece the bear meat; nothing would be wasted. All that Yahweh provides is used to its fullest.

Good First prepared a large portion to gift to the Pokanoket Tribe. They made a travois from small saplings of oak branches to pull the load with ease. Both Rainbow Warrior and Good First noticed they worked well together in this task. Smiles and giggles accompanied the work; they both sensed the beginning of friendship.

Good First decided in his heart and mind right there and then that Rainbow Warrior would be his bride one day.

Good First insisted on walking her back to Wellnomuck. Their conversation flowed as if they had always known each other and as if they always would. Silent moments were also comfortable for them both. The comfort they felt between each other formed a bond of trust in its baby beginnings. Through the years they both learned to nurture that trust in word and deed.

When reaching Wellnomuck, Good First gifted the Sagamore, It Thunders, who was Rainbow Warrior's father, with a large portion of bear meat. Awkwardly, but with determination, he spoke to Rainbow Warrior's father, the Sagamore, of his intention to have Rainbow Warrior as his bride in time, if she would have him and she and he approved.

Over the next thirteen moons he proved himself honorable. Rainbow Warrior accepted his invitation to become his wife.

The joining of Rainbow Warrior and Good First united two great peoples, the Nipmuc and Pokanoket. The two tribes became allies with each other. She thanked Yahweh for the many blessings she had received through the husband Yahweh had provided for her.

Rainbow Warrior began drumming very lightly and sang to Yahweh a prayer asking Yahweh to speak through her today. She also asked in song that Yahweh prepare hearts and minds to receive the wisdom from Him through her. Waves of Yahweh's love and kindness encircled her mind, body, and soul. She began to sing, "Come, come and gather, come, young and old. Come, come and gather to hear what I was told from Yahweh. Our Yahweh, He is near, Yahweh our Yahweh, come hear wisdom from Yahweh, come hear with your heart and your ears." Her voice was soothing, and dynamic lows and high tones were released without effort.

Rainbow Warrior sang this four times through, representing the four directions: North, South, East, and West. When she had completed the fourth round, all the village young and old had gathered and were seated, attentive to hear what Rainbow Warrior had received from Yahweh. She would be the vessel Yahweh used to bless the people, which included herself, with His wisdom. Her mandate was to teach the next seven generations as Yahweh was teaching her.

In the spring we the people of the Pokanoket Tribe meet to speak of the wisdom received at that time in our history; this is the prophecy that is coming to pass beginning that very day in Wellnomuck.

Rainbow Warrior ended the gathering song with seven

honor beats that are different from the double beat, the heartbeat of the song. The single loud beats are to honor Yahweh's presence.

All the people remained still and attentive in reverence to the presence of Yahweh. The air was thick with Yahweh's presence and His love. There was silence as the people raised their hands to worship the Creator of all things.

Chapter 6: I Need to Hear Your Voice

Chapter 7: Knowledge and Wisdom

Rainbow Warrior raised her head gracefully and spoke. "Yahweh is here. He is going to release knowledge and wisdom to us today. He has prepared our hearts and minds to receive His Good Spirit. He asks us to listen to His words released through me today. I am listening also. He asks us to speak these words often, to remind each other of His ways and how we are to live and love. He wants us to teach His ways to the next seven generations. Seven is the number of perfections. If each generation passes to seven generations the wisdom and knowledge that Yahweh gives us, it would be passed on eternally. This is a fundamental truth that Yahweh is giving to the Pokanoket people."

There was honored silence from all the community; even babies did not cry. This was a beautiful affirmation that Yahweh is present and is meeting everyone's needs.

Rainbow Warrior looked from face to face. As she spoke, her body flowed in movements so graceful and poised which expressed the effect of being in communion with the subject of all wisdom, Yahweh.

"Yahweh says we all must acknowledge Him as Creator of all things and honor Him above all things. We are to honor Him by honoring all His creation, the sun, moon, stars, the air, the flying things, the furred things, the creeping and crawling, and most importantly all peoples. But He is honored above all and before all. He expects us to take responsibility and do good with all He has given us. To multiply in goodness as He is good. To be thankful to Him in all things and for all things. We are to examine our hearts. We are to speak to our hearts ask our hearts, are we committed to do this today?"

There was complete silence. Rainbow Warrior continued, "Yahweh will not force this on anyone. He will only invite us to honor Him. That is all for today; ponder and speak to Him. Speak to your loved ones today of that which Yahweh requests. We will meet again as He leads us by the Spirit of Yahweh, in this season when He calls us to be His own. Aquene, (peace be with you.)" The tribal members began departing in small family groups. There was very little talking among the adults. The children did as all children do; they ran and jumped, gathered in groups making decisions on what they would do next, after chores were completed.

Everyone, in an orderly and purposeful manner, left the gathering. There was peace amongst the Pokanoket.

It Thunders, the Sagamore, Rainbow Warrior's father, the leader of all the bands of the Pokanoket, stayed behind. He waited until it was just he, Rainbow Warrior, and Good First at the great fire.

Sagamore, Peelha'quon (It Thunders), was a giant of a man with soft brown eyes, and long dark hair that he wore without braids. It fell to his midback and had streaks of white throughout. He smiled, and when he spoke his voice reflected his name. Each word he spoke, and his presence, demanded respect. The depth of his voice and his size showed a giant of a man. Good First, also a large man, was only shoulder height to him. Good First and Sagamore took hold of each other's right forearm and greeted each other saying, "A'ho, Aquene (I acknowledge you with honor, peace be with you)." Then with tender humility Sagamore bowed at his waist towards Rainbow Warrior and said, "Noonantam Weetompas, (blessing, my daughter,) the gathering was good. The people are ready to receive all that Yahweh has for them. Thank you for listening to Yahweh and telling us what Yahweh wants us to know."

Rainbow Warrior bowed toward the Sagamore, smiled, and said, "Kawanamush (I love you) and I love Yahweh. Yahweh loves us more than we can imagine. He will continue to talk and guide us so we may pass His goodness, knowledge, and wisdom to the next seven generations."

The three said their goodbyes. Sagamore stood and watched Rainbow Warrior and Good First walk hand and hand East towards their longhouse. His thoughts were of gratefulness and that all the people were blessed to have this couple as leaders in their nation. He prayed that Yahweh would continue to bless them all as all used their gifts to benefit all.

Chapter 7: Knowledge and Wisdom

Chapter 8:
THE DREAM

Rainbow Warrior and Good First walked hand and hand toward their longhouse in silence for some time until Rainbow Warrior spoke, "Husband, your dream; please tell me what Yahweh has shown you in your sleep time."

Good First stopped, faced his wife, and smiled. He spoke. "Yahweh spoke and showed me this, my love." Good First looked at Rainbow Warrior with great seriousness, yet there was a softness in his eyes. "He appeared to me as a great light, brighter than the sun, moon, or stars. There was the warmth of His love that soothed my soul, and peace, perfect peace. His voice was as many waters flowing in me and around me. He is all that is good and true and all of me heard Him say, 'The first will be the last and the last will be the first.' Yahweh said our people have found favor with Him. Yahweh said not to fear suffering; with great pain comes great outcome.

Our people would have a great impact on many nations and many peoples. I saw many nations, many peoples all together in the place we go after the great transition. He said to remain at peace, to live by His Spirit, and to accept the Word that also brings life. He will bring the Word to us. Then He said this, 'The Word is alive; the Word is a man; the Word is My Son. You have my Spirit; I now give you My Son.' He said, Rainbow Warrior, that HE would meet you. His Son would meet you at Wunne Sowams, soon and very soon."

Rainbow Warrior did not speak. She took every word into her heart and mind; as she did her spirit leaped within her. They embraced in silence until One Who Makes All Laugh appeared smiling. "Do you want to see my new dance?" As with one voice Good First and Rainbow Warrior said jubilantly, "Yes, yes, we do."

Their youngest grandson began twirling, jumping, and rolling on the ground. He began giggling as he did his dance. His giggle was so infectious that they all began giggling. Their giggles turned into laughter. This went on for several minutes until One Who Makes All Laugh suddenly stopped and said very seriously,

"Enough, there are chores to be done." He broke his seriousness and started giggling again. "Only kidding." They all laughed so hard and long that their faces began to hurt.

"Let us join the rest of the family now, little one, it is almost time for our midday meal," Rainbow Warrior said between giggles. They walked back to the longhouse, enjoying each moment being together.

Chapter 9:

Being Part of a Family

They met the rest of the family in the longhouse. Sunshine, their younger daughter, was preparing the meal for everyone to enjoy. Their older daughter, Fawn, was busy making new moccasins for Rainbow Fern, Fire Walker, and One Who Makes All Laugh. As she sewed the moccasins with sinew and porcupine quill, she thought, *They all seem to be growing out of moccasins every moon.* The men had made their way to get materials to make arrows. They intently gathered the right stone, the right branches and feathers. Their family worked together to meet all their needs. Their home was full of laughter, love, and peace.

Rainbow Warrior combed and braided all her grandchildren's hair each night. They played a game Rainbow Warrior made up called Find the Porcupine

Quill. She was so quick and elusive in braiding a quill into one of the children's hair they never caught on to whose hair it was braided in. Each child had one guess in whose hair the quill would be found. The winner would get a bit of honey and pine needle, a treat they all loved.

"Who has the quill?" Rainbow Warrior peered at each of her grandchildren and poked each one softly in the stomach. "Is it you, you, or you?" and burst into laughter.

"I think it is me," Fire Walker shouted.

"I think it is Fire Walker also," Rainbow Fern said with a smile. One Who Makes All Laugh stood up, swirled in a circle, did a little jump and a wiggle, and sang in a deep made-up voice, "Well, I think it is me." Everyone laughed, and Rainbow Warrior, with a flip of her hand, pulled the quill from Fire Walker's hair.

"Aw..." One Who Makes All Laugh made an over-emphasized frown which made everyone laugh.

Rainbow Warrior prepared the honey and pine in small gourd bowls for the winners. As she left them, she said, "Now prepare yourself for bed and to see Uruttatchikkeasasin (Grandfather) for your blessing."

As she left her grandchildren, she looked back to see that Fire Walker and Rainbow Fern both took a bit of their winnings and put it into another gourd, then they both handed it to One Who Makes All laugh. He smiled and hugged them both, "Katobotash (thank you). Kawanamush (I love you)." They all said in unison, "Katobatash kukummus, Kawanamush, (Thank you, Grandmother, I love you)." Rainbow Warrior's heart was filled with joy as she saw how well her grandchildren cared for each other.

Chapter 10:
The Blessing

The children prepared for their blessing from Grandfather. Their blessing would happen in two parts, first individually, then they all would meet together with Grandfather to receive a corporate blessing. This nightly event had taken place as long as any of the children could remember. Rightly so, for Good First had blessed each child every night since the day they were born.

Rainbow Fern, being the oldest, would receive her blessing first. Grandfather was sitting at a small fire in an area of the long house that was used to sit and chat.

Good First was sitting on furs on the ground, a small fire in front of him. Rainbow Fern walked up to Good First, folded her legs beneath her body, and curled up in his lap, never losing eye contact with her grandfather. Good First thought Rainbow Fern's tiny frame, tawny skin, and long amber hair made her look so like her grandmother. Rainbow Fern, being very direct, could make ordinary conversation sound like great wisdom. "I am ready, Grandfather."

"Indeed you are, Rainbow Fern. You are your grandmother's and my first grandchild; your blessings come with great abilities and great burdens. You will be able to discern changes in the atmosphere, moods, and frequencies. Yahweh will teach you to fight in prayer; you will pray your cousins into their manhood as you are growing into your womanhood. You will be able to find your way on any path. You will hear Yahweh's voice before you say, 'Follow me, this is the way you are to go.'

Yahweh has given you so many gifts, and with each gift will come responsibility and pain, dear one. These burdens are lightened to that of a feather when you give back to Yahweh that which He gives you. You shall succeed! This is your blessing." Good First pulled Rainbow Fern into his chest, kissed her head, and said, "Sleep well and dream, dreams spoken to you by Creator. Now send in Fire Walker."

Rainbow Fern rose from her grandfather's lap, never losing eye contact. Her eyes spoke so clearly, she need not use words. She conveyed her love by the way she softened her eyes. She looked at her grandfather so lovingly he was filled with warmth, and smiled. She simply nodded her head as she left her grandfather's presence to go tell Fire Walker it was his turn for his blessing.

Fire Walker was sitting on furs by the central fire, his eyes fixed on the dancing yellow, red, orange, blue and white flames. He rose and turned toward Rainbow Fern before she spoke. They fixed their eyes on each other, they nodded as they passed and at the same time said, "Kawanamush, I love you."

Rainbow Fern's voice was soft and rhythmic, like a running stream. She asked, "Where is One Who Makes All Laugh? "

Fire Walker answered, smiling, "Lil guy wore himself out entertaining us; he is in his bedding. Good anticipating, Rainbow Fern!"

These types of words were spoken often in the Pokanoket homes, words of encouragement. Saying kawanamush (I love you) helped everyone to do and be their best.

****

I, Harvest Moon, using hands gestures as I am speaking, move my right arm towards the left side of the room then gracefully to the right. I look to the left side of the community center, then to the right. Softening my eyes, I move slowly and make eye contact as I speak.

"Yesterday's behaviors are to be brought into today's life. These words of affirmation were common in Rainbow Warrior's day. Each year at this time we are reminded to continue to verbalize our love and affirmation, to help each become our best. This is a very serious byproduct of the Pokanoket culture. To build each other up individually is to build the whole Pokanoket Tribe."

Several people nodded or smiled as she spoke. "This story is to remind us to make this behavior tangible in our everyday lives. Pokanoket are to show love, kindness, and honor. Pokanoket are to show love in word and deed, day in and day out, for the betterment of all.

"We are not a perfect people, but we are gifted with the Holy Spirit of Yahweh. His character is ingrained in our DNA. We are to fight every conflict, large and small, on our knees with our hands raised in adoration to Yahweh. Yahweh has given us all we need to be successful, forgiveness and His Son Yeshua. We are asked today to continue to seek the way of 'the beginning place', in the great garden told to us by the elders, the place where no darkness dwelt. This place has been hidden because of disobedience. The Pokanoket strive for obedience, admitting mistakes, allowing the Spirit of Yahweh to lead them in their words and deeds. This behavior has kept the Pokanoket Tribe blessed under Yahweh's covering."

The people, young and old, continue to smile and nod their heads in agreement as they listen. My eyes peruse the community. "I will continue the prophecy where I left off.

****

Fire Walker approached Good First with a soft smile and soft eyes. As he knelt, they grasped right forearms and looked deeply into each other's eyes as if searching for a treasure.

Fire Walker and Good First continued to gaze at each other, not at what is seen physically but looking deeper as if into each other's DNA. They looked deep into each other's spirit.

Good First spoke, his voice deep and soothing. "Grandson Fire Walker, you are doing well in your training as fire keeper. I have seen this with my own eyes and heard from the elders that you have been designed by Yahweh to do this. Do you know this?"

Fire Walker and Good First continued clasping forearms. Relaxed, yet keeping a posture of respect, he answered, "Yes Uruttatchikkensasin (Grandfather), this I do know."

Good First leaned in ever so slightly and said, "I will now speak your blessing."

Fire Walker tightened his grasp on his grandfather's forearm.

"Your blessings are going to pour into you like the spring rain pours into the land. Fire Walker, you will pour out what you receive for the good of everyone. As a waterfall cannot be contained, neither shall your blessings. Your blessings will flow like the current of the river. They shall not stop flowing through you; they are to help others. Fire Walker, you will be given wisdom and knowledge in every situation; have no fear even when there is danger. Fire Walker, you will be led by Yahweh to walk through many fires. Fire Walker, you will know nothing will harm you, because you never walk alone. Yahweh is close at hand.

"I see both water and fire working in you, and I see

how together this blessing will bless all." They sat in silence for several minutes. Their faces in the dimness of fires' light glowed as the Spirit of Yahweh rested on them.

"Grandson." Good First leaned forward until their foreheads touched. "Do not move out of fear, do not fear even at your death, do not fear. Yahweh has everything and everyone moving as He and only He directs… just know He has already finished. This is your blessing."

Fire Walker and Good First rose from sitting. They continued to grasp each other's forearm and look directly in each other's eyes.

"Thank you, Grandfather, I will send in One Who Make All Laugh." Fire Walker waited for Good First to release his hold of his arm before he moved.

Good First did not speak or move, but Fire Walker could feel his grandfather's essence walk with him to the fire. He saw the essence of his grandfather in the form of light and sound go into the fire.

Suddenly, Fire Walker was in a vision of the realm in which Yahweh dwells. Fire Walker was brought into eternity, where time is not measured. He walked amongst all his relations that had passed over with fire and water and all his grandfather said was confirmed. All was revealed to him even as he continued to retrieve One Who Makes All Laugh from his nap.

Chapter 11:

Peace Will Show You the Way

Good First pondered the birth of One Who Makes All Laugh. He came early, one moon earlier than expected. He came with gushes of water and was so small that Sunshine never had to push to deliver him. It was as if he rode in on a wave of birthing water.

Good First remembered how small this baby was; his whole body fit in the palm of Good First's hand. Babies that size are not expected to survive, but Sunshine said (and all agreed) she would not bring this child to the crying rocks. The Crying Rocks is the place women would say their final goodbyes to babies that did not survive.

As the baby was brought to Sunshine's breast to feed, he laughed loud and long. No child in the Pokanoket Tribe had ever been known to do this minutes after birth.

His dark eyes were wide open and though small, he held his head up and laughed again. Everyone stopped, looked at each other, and began to laugh until their sides hurt.

A very tense moment changed in a second as this peculiar baby that had a gift to make others laugh came into this world. His mother named him then, and all agreed his name was One Who Makes All Laugh.

Fire Walker met with Rainbow Fern and One Who Makes All Laugh in their sleeping area. "Come, brother, grandfather is waiting to bless you this evening." One Who Makes All laugh did a tumble and a jump and made his way to his grandfather.

Approaching his grandfather, he smiled and said, "Grandfather, I am here; you have saved the best till last."

He wiggled his way over to grandfather, sat facing him, and took both his grandfather's hands into his. This naturally put a smile on Good First's face; he felt light and at peace.

With a look of resolve Good First said, "Your blessing is in a sense the best, for your blessing is that you can bring all to their best. You will deposit peace in exchange for fear, love for hate, light for darkness. My grandson, you will bring peace wherever you go. This peace will guide the people. This is your blessing."

"A'ho, Grandfather, I agree. Shall I get the others for our unity blessing?"

"Yes, little one," Grandfather said. Immediately, One Who Makes All Laugh yelled, "It is time for our unity blessing. Hurry up, Rainbow Fern; hurry up, Fire Walker." This gesture made the whole household burst into laughter, just as he did the day he was born. Peace filled their home.

Chapter 12:
BETTER TOGETHER

Rainbow Fern and Fire Walker returned to the small fire where One Who Makes All Laugh and their grandfather were sitting. Rainbow Fern and Fire Walker sat next to One Who Makes All Laugh; they naturally reached for each other's hands.

Grandfather took a moment to look at each child. "Creator has favored you. You are each like a straight oak stick," Grandfather said as he picked up a straight oak stick that he had placed by his side earlier. "Alone, this stick is easily broken." Good First took the stick; held each end, placed it against his knee, then pulled on each end. There was a snapping sound when the stick broke. Good First was now holding two pieces of oak stick, one in each hand. Good First looked at his grandchildren, picked up three oak sticks, and said, "Did you see how easily one stick is broken?"

Good First took all three oak sticks and wrapped them together tightly with sinew. He took the bound sticks by the ends, brought them to his knee, and pulled hard on each end of the sticks. The three sticks stayed intact even as Good First made great effort to break the sticks. One Who Makes All Laugh, Fire Walker, and Rainbow Fern kept their eyes fixed on their grandfather.

Good First said, "This is your blessing. I have shown you that one stick is easily broken. I am not able to break these three sticks bound together so tightly.

"Stay united; unity is your blessing. Do all things with this in mind. You are better together, stronger together, safer together. Unity will always be a blessing. Now give me hugs and kisses and go say your prayers with Grandmother. You will have dreams of strengthening each other. I love you."

At the same time, all three said, "We love you; thank you, grandfather, sleep well."

The three got up, gave hugs and kisses to Good First, and walked together holding hands to their grandmother's sleeping area. Rainbow Warrior was sitting on her bedding, braiding her hair.

A sudden gush of cool air entered their longhouse. Rainbow Warrior felt the cool breeze as fresh spring night air entered the longhouse. She looked to the longhouse's flap and saw the flap was open. The Sagamore, It Thunders, entered, his eyes looking sullen and strained. He stood at the opening and said in a loud, yet gentle voice, "Gives Well has transitioned to the spirit world."

Gives Well was the brother of Good First and the husband of Rainbow Warrior's sister, Dragon Fly. Good First and Rainbow Warrior both walked over to the Sagamore and directed him to sit on the deer hide close to the central fire. There was a stillness in their longhouse.

Fawn spoke up, for the whole household had heard the news of Gives Well's transitioning to the great mystery when Sagamore announced it upon entering.

"Sunshine and I will finish praying with the children. The men will bring firewood to Dragon Fly's longhouse tonight; they will start Gives Well's transitioning fire and see if she and the children have any other immediate needs." Fawn said this with compassion and authority, her gifts in action.

Sunshine and Fawn had arms around the children, leading them to their sleeping area, comforting them on the way, their gifts in action.

Smiling Wind and Tethers Close proceeded to exit to their assignment, to start Gives Well's transition fire. When passing It Thunders, Good First, and Rainbow Warrior they touched each shoulder, eyes lowered. They both said, "Praying Yahweh's comfort," the night air entering as they exited the longhouse, their gifts in action.

The atmosphere was heavy and still. Rainbow Warrior, Good First, and the Sagamore sat near the smoldering fire; the only sound heard was the crackling of the fire. The three sat, legs crossed, holding each other's hand for several minutes before the Sagamore spoke.

His size seemed to have diminished; the sadness was evident in his posturing. His shoulders, usually wide and broad, were now rounded and sunken, his face facing down towards his chest. Sagamore's thunderous voice was now more like a gentle breeze.

"Gives Well woke long enough to request that you, Good First, care for the spiritual needs of his children. All the Pokanoket will provide for their every physical need. Are you willing to father Gives Well's children?"

Without hesitation, Good First said, "I will care for Rides on Wind, Tender Bear, and Screeching Bird. They are our close relations; we love them." They sat in silence for several minutes until Good First said, "Shall we ask Yahweh to exchange joy for this sadness, as only He can?" Both Rainbow Warrior and Sagamore said, "A'ho, we agree."

Good First's tears flowed in a steady stream as he thanked Creator Yahweh for his brother and friend's life.

"Creator, thank You that Gives Well lived well; thank You for welcoming him home where there is no longer struggle or pain. As his transitioning fire burns may we be reminded of the greatest mystery, Your love. When Your love called him, Gives Well answered. Give us wisdom and strength as we go through our suffering. We thank You for covering his widow and his children with every comfort needed. Great One, Maker of All Things, equip me with the love and skills to be the father to my brother's three children. They are our close relations; mesh us deeper in Your love."

Good First put his head into his hands and wept. He made no sound, but his tears flowed like a river.

After some time, he lifted his head and took a deep breath. In his heart's ear he could hear his brother, Gives Well, say, "Thank you, brother, for taking my arrows and adding them to your quiver." Good First could smell the scent of pine and honey so clean and sweet in the air as he heard these words within and without.

It Thunders and Rainbow Warrior sat on either side of Good First, each touching a shoulder. They both recognized the clean and sweet smell of pine and honey. They silently prayed for Yahweh to comfort, strengthen, and to give them more love.

****

Chapter 13:
Come to Comfort

I, Harvest Moon, stop speaking, I tilt my head to the left, as if I did, I would hear better. I look across the entire room, I soften my eyes and graciously speak in a melodic tone, resuming the story.

****

Rainbow Warrior said "More love, more of Your love, Creator. We are all feeling great grief; we know that with more of Your love we will prosper even in our time of grief." Good First and It Thunders together said, "A'ho."

The Sagamore rose from sitting. "I will stay with Walks Well at Gives Well's transition fire. Word will go out from Drum Rock to your family the Nipmuc, along with Pequot, Narragansett, and Niantic. They will pass on to the Mohawk, Mohegan, Delaware, Shinnecock, and others the news of Gives Well's departure from here to the great mystery." As he spoke, the sound of the message being sent out from Drum Rock was heard. "There will be family and friends coming soon to honor his family and his life. A'ho."

Sagamore turned and walked to exit the longhouse. His height appeared diminished, his shoulders sunken, his head low in visible grief. The coolness of the night breeze entered again as Sagamore departed.

Rainbow Warrior and Good First rose. Without an exchange of words they reached for each other's hands. Rainbow Warrior's right hand, palm up, grasped Good First's left hand, palm down. Hand in hand, they walked to their sleeping area. Good First sat on the bedding, lifted his legs onto the bed and lay down. He looked at Rainbow Warrior, then looked at the valley at his left side where his wife lay every night. His eyes beckoned her to lay beside him. Rainbow Warrior fulfilled her husband's unspoken request, lying on her right side, her head on his welcoming left shoulder. Her left arm lay on Good First's bare chest and her left leg rested comfortably over his left leg. In this embrace they felt that it was not easy to see where one started or finished, for the two had become as one. In each other's arms, the couple entered prayer, thanking Yahweh for being their joy and peace. They drifted into sleep remaining in their embrace. Dreams of the place where

Yahweh dwells filled their minds. They had visitations of relatives who had transitioned in years past, who exuded love. They both entered the same dream, seeing their dear brother and friend Gives Well walking towards a most beautiful land.

Gives Well looked back and smiled; his appearance was lovely indeed, more lovely than any could be in this realm. He waved and smiled, which dispersed the essence of love into the atmosphere. Gives Well turned back to the path he was walking on, his presence getting harder to see. The feeling of his love increased in the hearts and minds of Good First and Rainbow Warrior even as they slept.

Rainbow Warrior opened her eyes and lay in her husband gentle embrace in quiet prayer, thanking Yahweh for keeping her, her family, and tribe through the night. She loosened herself from her husband's cradled arm without waking him, as she did most mornings. She rested her right hand on Good First chest to feel his heartbeat and prayed, "Yahweh, comfort him, strengthen him, direct him to do what You see is good."

She looked towards the center fire and saw that Sunshine had made morning provision. She knew that Sunshine had done this because she drew a sun on the ground and placed the provision in front of it. This put a smile on Rainbow Warrior's face. Rainbow Warrior also noticed that her bag with her prayer elements was at the exit to the longhouse, her shawl folded neatly over her bag. This also caused a smile.

Rainbow Warrior walked past the center fire. The warmth of the embers touched the bare skin of her face and arms. In a soft whisper she prayed, "Yahweh, thank You for Your provision; You give and take away. I am grateful that you have given us Your love and protection."

Picking up her elements and shawl with her right hand and pushing out the flap to the longhouse, Rainbow Warrior stepped out into the cool morning air.

The moon was full and there was the familiar smell of smoke from all the longhouses and the community fire. There was another fire burning, outside Gives Well's and Dragon Fly's dwelling: Gives Well's transitioning fire. The fire had yellow, red and white flames that looked as if they were dancing in the early morning moonlight. There were several people sitting and standing around the fire. One of the figures standing at the fire made Rainbows Warrior's spirit leap. Running Brook, her and Dragon Fly's younger sister, had returned to Sowams from up North in Heron country. She had not returned in seven full seasons; she had not yet met One Who Makes All Laugh. Rainbow Warrior with gratefulness thanked Yahweh. "We are one again. All my sisters are here at Sowams."

Chapter 13: Come to Comfort

Rainbow Warrior breathed in and out deeply and moved with determination to the path that lead to Potumtuk. She walked with confidence; she had walked this path for many, many seasons.

The thoughts of Gives Well's demise happening here because of a slip, a fall, and hitting his head on a rock entered her mind. Rainbow Warrior wondered how long Gives Well had lain there before he was found. Why was he even here; where was he going or coming from? The questions of how her brother-in-law was found bloodied and unconscious on the path to Potumtuk played havoc with Rainbow Warrior's thoughts this morning.

She heard in her spirit the voice of Yahweh saying, "Trust Me." The sound of Creator's voice settled her spirit.

"I trust You, Yahweh; in all things, I trust You." Rainbow Warrior said this and let herself focus on the path ahead, walking fervently towards Potumtuk.

She smelled the salt in the air and heard the rhythmic sounds of the waves coming to shore. Rainbow Warrior could tell that the tide was going out by the sound of the waves.

She entered the circled area from the East and sat on her knees, facing North. She mixed and lit the cedar, sage and sweetgrass that she placed in a large quohog shell.

Peace enveloped her. She placed the shell on the ground in front of her and raised her arm over her head. With humility of heart she spoke.

"Yahweh, I'm here. I love You and thank You for loving me. I am so grateful for Your care for us and all Your creation. I come to You asking You to use me for Your good pleasure. Show me how to live and move and have my being." Rainbow Warrior was confident that Yahweh would answer her. He had every time she set time aside for Him.

Suddenly before Rainbow Warrior there was light and fire so bright that nothing else could be seen but this. She continued to feel peace, the peace only the Creator can deposit. Creator changes the atmosphere.

Then Creator spoke audibly. Rainbow Warrior had never heard Creator with her ears before; He had always spoken to her internally, through her heart's ear. But today she heard Him audibly; His voice sounded like many rushing waters. Creator said, "Tomorrow, come with your sisters to the seashore. Take the path from here to the water's edge. Do not come alone tomorrow; tomorrow bring Running Brook and Dragon Fly. My son Yeshua will meet you there. I have already met with Running Brook and Dragon Fly in a dream. Rainbow Warrior, you will confirm that the dream was of Me when you see your sisters today. Go back to Wellamuck now; go in peace."

Rainbow Warrior rose to her feet and gathered her things; she had learned to act in immediate obedience to Yahweh. She learned that obedience is lifegiving.

Rainbow Warrior was filled with amazement from the brilliance of the light, the fire, and the sound of Creator's voice. The fire did not burn anything, yet had radiating heat that warmed and penetrated her heart. Though she had heard His voice audibly for the first time, His voice was oh so familiar. The encounter deposited peace that strengthened her soul.

She closed her eyes; she was still as Yahweh spoke again. This time, she didn't hear Him audibly but what Yahweh said was just as clear in her heart's ear.

"Rainbow Warrior, I will take you home; you will ride beneath My wing, dear one." His voice now sounded like the wind.

Chapter 14:
The One of Many Names

Rainbow Warrior had no recollection of her flight back home. She remembered standing up and then she found herself at the flap of Dragon Fly's longhouse. The peace she felt kept her focused on her next step.

Rainbow Warrior entered Dragon Fly's longhouse. Around the center fire sat her two sisters, Running Brook the younger and Shining Dragon Fly the elder. Both Dragon Fly and Running Brook had long, dark brown hair that they wore in one braid that cascaded down their backs to below their waistlines. Their skin was smooth, tawny brown, and youthful.

Her sisters looked to Rainbow Warrior. The Spirit of Yahweh was speaking to all three, depositing the same word and vision. They all saw Gives Well walking on the path towards Potumtuk on the night he died. They heard him singing Yahweh's song. He said in a loud voice, "I am willing." They saw him fall and hit his head on a rock. There was a gush of blood, white light, and a feeling of peace.

They reached out to hold each other's hands and walked over to sit on deer hides at the central fire. Rainbow Warrior was the first to speak. "I met with Yahweh this morning. He said that He had given you both instructions." As Rainbow Warrior spoke, they felt the Spirit of Yahweh's unconditional love wrapped around them. They all took in a deep breath in awe of His manifest love. When they exhaled, they had visions of angelic beings being released into the atmosphere.

Yahweh's presence entered the longhouse; the center fire glowed in white, blue, and purple flames. His voice was like many winds, rushing waters, thunder, and fire. They all entered His peace that strengthened their souls.

Yahweh spoke. "He will come on the ocean waters. Meet My Son tomorrow at Potumtuk. Angels have been assigned to you and yours. Do not fear. I am who I am; I am He that provides your every need. I know the end from beginning. You have known me as Yahweh. I am Sagamore of Sagamore, Chief of Chiefs; I am the lover of your soul, Creator of All Things; I am the Bright Morning Star. I am all you will ever need. Now, eat and rest. Tomorrow you will meet My Son. He and I are one."

The sisters postured to worship. With arms reaching towards the sky, they humbly received instruction as they thanked Yahweh for His presence. Together they took a deep breath and exhaled. Peace and love like a thin cloud was visible; a very fine mist was felt on their faces and arms.

Rainbow Warrior took her older sisters' hands and said, "Three more days the fire will burn for your husband. Are all your needs being met?"

Dragon Fly answered, "Would you be with me as I dress Gives Well before his spirit is released to Yahweh?"

Running Brook spoke, "I will not leave your side. Rainbow Warrior, you come as you can; your best help now is to meet the children's needs. Is this a good plan, Dragon Fly?"

Dragon Fly answered, "Yes, thank you, sisters. Let's nourish ourselves and rest as we have been instructed. We will come to you tomorrow morning, Rainbow Warrior. Then we three will walk together to Potumtuk."

Family and friends had been bringing food since word came of Gives Well's demise. There was provision at the center fire of venison stew, quail, fiddle heads, berries, honey, and gourds of water. They each thanked Yahweh for His provision and ate.

Rainbow Warrior took Running Brook's hand; she squeezed it and smiled. "Sister, you have not met my youngest grandson, One Who Makes All Laugh."

No sooner did she voice these words than One Who Makes All Laugh peeked through the opening of Dragon Fly's longhouse. He stepped just inside the door. Looking at his grandmother and great aunts, he smiled and said, "Sometimes we laugh, sometimes we cry; we will do both for Gives Well. Running Brook, I am your youngest relation. May we embrace?"

Rainbow Warrior was pleasantly surprised by the maturity of her youngest grandchild. Running Brook smiled. "Come, child."

One Who Makes All Laugh did sommersaults over to Running Brook. Laughter filled the air; another wave of peace entered all their hearts and minds.

Hugs and kisses were passed out as Running Brook and One Who Makes All Laugh sat together. They exchanged questions and answers, as they purposely got to know each other. The two bonded immediately.

Hours passed. The four ate, rested, had times of quietness, laughter, and tears just as One Who Makes All Laugh had said. At dusk Rainbow Warrior said it was time to take One Who Makes All Laugh home for his evening blessing. Hugs and kisses were exchanged before Rainbow Warrior and One Who Makes All Laugh lifted the flap and entered the early spring night air.

Chapter 15: Embracing Change

Rainbow Warrior and One Who Makes All Laugh walked home hand in hand. The sky was deep blue and purple, as the sun had dipped beneath the horizon. The air was cool; the sounds of night creatures so familiar and soothing. They took in all the familiar aromas of home: wood burning, food cooking, cedar, sage and sweetgrass, as well as the faint smell of pine needles and honey representing every healing measure needed for any situation.

Both honey and pine have healing properties; joining the two makes another whole, which is better than either one alone.

No words were exchanged on their walk home, only smiles and a squeeze of their hands. They both sensed change without questioning it; peace filled their hearts.

Entering their longhouse, One Who Makes All Laugh loosened his hand from Rainbow Warrior's. "Kawanamush, Grandmother. I am going to join the others for our blessings."

He ran to his sleeping area to meet his siblings and cousins. Rainbow Warrior embraced the change as a gift from Yahweh. She watched as One Who Makes All Laugh scampered to meet the other children.

Then Rainbow Warrior entered a vision, into the realm where time does not exist. She saw seeds that were planted in the soil. In darkness, she knew, the seeds die; with the death of the seeds there is the struggle of change. That struggle produces a seedling. Yahweh's provision in the time of darkness gives strength to the seedlings. This strength enables the seedling to push past the darkness to the light of the sun. Yahweh produces and gives the light of the sun and water from the rain. The seedling grows to maturity.

She also was shown seed buried that just died. Though planted the same, somewhere in the process there was a disconnect with Yahweh, which led to the seed's death. The revelation given to Rainbow Warrior was that to live we must remain connected to Yahweh. Rainbow Warrior sensed Yahweh telling her a healthy, mature plant will reproduce thirty, sixty or a hundred times, but only if the heart of the seed remained in Yahweh and in His will.

She received great understanding of the position of one's heart. Life comes when hearts remain in Yahweh's will. Anything out of Yahweh's will is death.

Being obedient to Him will produce life, while disobedience produces death. Yahweh will not force obedience; He gives everyone the choice of which path they will walk.

The vision and revelation happened with no lapse in time; she continued to follow One Who Makes All Laugh to the children's sleeping area.

Good First, her daughters, their husbands, and her grandchildren, along with Rides on Wind, Tender Bear, and Screeching Bird were all in the children's sleeping area. She noticed the children's sleeping area had been adapted to provide beds for Rides on Wind, Tender Bear, and Screeching Bird. This was a change noted and embraced.

Good First greeted his bride, Rainbow Warrior, with tender kisses on her forehead. His arms naturally found their way about her waist.

Good First lifted his left arm; his right arm remained around Rainbow Warriors waist. "Yahweh has spoken to me with a new blessing to speak over all of you, dear ones. He is adding three to three: a double blessing. Adding Yahweh makes the number seven, which is perfection."

"Rides on Wind, Rainbow Fern, Yahweh has given you His heart. Nurture this gift with love and prayer and you will also release angels to do His will. Passion will provide you with purpose; you will endure many things with joy to meet a great ending."

Good First continued speaking. "Fire

Walker, One Who Makes All Laugh, Tender Bear, Screeching Bird, you will be gatekeepers over the four directions.

One Who Makes All Laugh, you will be the gatekeeper to the North. The color white is yours." When he spoke to his youngest grandson, he naturally smiled. "One Who Makes All Laugh, you will laugh at darkness. You will shine the light of Yahweh, and darkness will not be able to exist in this light. You will encourage and teach others to do the same; this will produce peace."

Good First continued, now looking to Tender Bear. "Tender Bear, you will be the gatekeeper to the South; black is your color. Tender Bear, like the gentle southern winds come and warm us, you shall protect us as the battles become more intense. As if with the mighty arm of Yahweh fanning you along His designated path, you shall speak life over death; death will not prevail. This also will produce peace."

"Fire Walker, you shall take the Eastern Gate and

yellow is your color. Fire Walker, you will always be present, even if not seen. You will see in the spirit realm and speak what Yahweh is mandating. You will show us how to straighten the way for the coming of Yahweh. This is where the fire of purity and the continued cleansing waters shall pour out, never ending. This is to prepare the hearts of the people to meet Yahweh, for without this cleansing none could stand. This will produce peace."

"Screeching Bird, you shall man the Western Gate; your color is red. You are the youngest and the weakest physically. This is your blessing, for where we are weak, He is strong. The strength of Yahweh will manifest in your weakness. You will speak the heart of a good father over wayward sons and daughters. Many will return and be healed in their minds, bodies, and souls as you allow Yahweh to work through you, and this will produce peace.

"These blessings are in addition to all the blessings you have previously received. Yahweh will continue to pour out His will upon us as we all remain one. Stay in unity, lifting others before yourself. In this Yahweh sees no wrong. But if wrong occurs, quickly state it and turn from it; forgive, forgive quickly yourself and others. This will keep a united force. This is the blessing I speak over you that I have received from Yahweh.

"We, your parents, grandparents, and all our relations before us join in a united prayer to encourage and draw us all to our destinies in Yahweh."

With Good First's last words, all hands were lifted in adoration to Yahweh. Each expressed humility, gratefulness, and veneration. The presence of Yahweh filled their home with peace.

Fawn, Laughing Wind, Sunshine, and Tethers Close volunteered to finish the children's nighttime rituals, braiding their hair and taking care of last minute needs before they retired to their sleeping area. This was the first time Rainbow Warrior would not braid her grandchildren's hair before bed. She felt the shift of change and embraced it as good. She was tired and longed to be in the arms of her gift from Yahweh—her husband, Good First.

She and Good First made their way to their bedding to lay in each other's arms. They thanked Yahweh for this day and asked Him to watch over and meet them in their dreams.

They drifted off to sleep and met once again in a dream, where they also met their elders who had entered the cloud of great mystery with Yahweh. Yahweh watched with great pleasure as the elders in the cloud gave them invisible gifts that they knew were of great worth. They both woke suddenly with a gasp of air as if they saw something magnificent, then exhaling simultaneously. They felt the release of Yahweh's will into the atmosphere, and received what appeared to them as new eyes to see past the ordinary to the extraordinary. This was a change neither could have imagined, but they embraced it.

They lay facing each other, looking deeply into each other's eyes. No words were needed as their spirits agreed: love would show them the way and peace would guide them. Yahweh is love; in His presence there is peace.

Yahweh spoke to Rainbow Warrior in her heart's ear. She heard, "Wait for Dragon Fly and Running Brook and come to Potumtuk. Wait at the water's edge for My Son, Yeshua. We are one."

She was obedient to His direction and did not leave that morning to go to Potumtuk. In faith she embraced this change.

The morning was filled with prayer, food, laughter, and unity. They all did the things that came naturally for them to do, each used their gifts which also complimented the others' gifts. Though there were many present, they all worked together as one, accomplishing great tasks with ease.

Both Good First and Rainbow Warrior saw these things through the eyes that see beyond the veil, through the Spirit of Yahweh. They saw that all present had an angel that directed, protected and corrected them. They could see the love for Yahweh, the thankfulness to Yahweh, the promises, provision, and gifts of Yahweh. All the gifts from Yahweh had sound and color. His fire and breath filled their home.

Good First and Rainbow Warrior joined hands, prayed, worshipped, and thanked Yahweh for all they had. This was the only aspect of who they were that they were not willing to change. They agreed to this as a family: Yahweh is first in all things, always. This they would not change.

Chapter 16:
Three Sisters

Rainbow Warrior was drawn to the opening of the longhouse; she opened the flap just in time to meet her sisters Dragon Fly and Running Brook. Today they would walk together to Potumtuk.

Rainbow Warrior did not pick up her elements; she would be obedient to Yahweh and go to the water's edge to meet Yahweh's Son with her sisters. No cedar, sage or sweetgrass would be brought with her today. She knew that all veils had been lifted; love and truth were the tangible elements she would bring today.

Good First had walked to Rainbow Warrior from their sleeping area. He took his bride's hands in his, then with a gentle smile and a nod he released his bride to her sisters. A perfect gift to her this morning; she knew he would be praying for all of them and their time at Potumtuk.

Rainbow Warrior stepped out of the longhouse to the beauty of the day. The air was fresh and crisp, the sky the palest of blue without any clouds. All the familiar aromas of home met her nostrils along with the warmth of the rising bright yellow sun that touched her cheeks. She felt deep gratefulness for the gift of a new day.

The three sisters embraced. Dragon Fly said, "Shall we be on our way, sisters?" Rainbow Warrior and Running Brook nodded in agreement.

The three sisters enjoyed all creation, as all creation began their morning songs and dances to thank Yahweh for a new day: the bird songs, the rustling of the leaves, the wind as it passed through the leaves and the tall grasses. The sounds and movements were demonstrations of Yahweh's steadfast love. All creation, in their own way, gave praise to Yahweh, the Creator of all things. The sisters meditated on Yahweh's goodness as they walked the path, enjoying another day of life. Rainbow Warrior's thoughts were of Yahweh's mercy and grace that meets all creation each day.

There was no conversation as they walked up the incline to Potumtuk. The sisters silently prayed the entire way. They knew peace led them, love held them, and truth bound them. When they reached Potumtuk, they released a sound as they made their way down the narrow path to the ocean's edge. The three sisters' voices were simple and beautiful, singing, "Yah." The sound joined all creation praising Yahweh for another day.

They descended in order of birth, Dragon Fly leading, Rainbow Warrior followed by Running Brook, each step intentional as they kept their eyes on the rocky terrain.

The sound of rhythmic ocean waves hitting the shore and the smell of salt in the air cleared their minds as they moved slowly down the decline to meet the ocean's edge. It was not until all three were on the solid ground of the shoreline that they stopped singing and looked out to the horizon.

Five hundred feet off the shore they saw a canoe with

one man in it paddling towards shore.

The sisters took each other's hands and watched the man come in to about fifty feet from shore. The man had long brown hair, tan skin, hair on his face, and was dressed as the men dressed at home: in buckskin, leggings, and moccasins. He got out of the canoe and pulled it onto the shore, away from where the breaking waves could reach.

The sisters all thought there was nothing in this man's appearance that would draw one near, yet they all felt an inner pull to Him in the essence of their very being.

He walked to them with a beautiful smile on His face; He held out His arms to embrace them. Without hesitation, the three sisters moved closer to this man to receive His embrace as if He were a loved and respected family member. As He wrapped His arms around them, peace and love enveloped them.

Dragon Fly laughed out loud; Rainbow Warrior gasped like one who watched the wonder of birth, and tears of joy ran down Running Brook's face. His embrace felt like the warm summer sun wrapped around them and there was the sweet smell of pine and honey in the air.

The man stepped back, His smile so beautiful, His eyes kind. His embrace lingered on them, though He had stepped away.

"I am Yeshua; I am Yahweh's Son. We are one with

the Holy Spirit. Your people have known and revered Yahweh and the Holy Spirit. Now I have come to give you food that will sustain you in time of physical and spiritual need. I do only what I have seen Yahweh do and say only what He tells Me to say. Let us go sit at Potumtuk. A place has been prepared for us; follow Me."

He walked and spoke with authority as He made His way to the path upward to the peak of Potumtuk. The sisters followed Him in silence. Peace and confidence swelled in their hearts. The four climbed the incline up the path to view the place Rainbow Warrior had met with Yahweh year after year.

Yeshua entered the circle through the East Gate. In the center there was a fire burning, with fish cooking in a clay pot. There was also a clay pot cooking something they had never seen; it had an aroma the sisters were not familiar with. There were four gourds of cool, fresh spring water, one set at each direction. Yeshua sat North facing South, Rainbow Warrior sat South facing Yeshua.

Running Brook sat to the East and Dragon Fly facing her to the West.

Running Brook was first to speak. "Who prepared this? It was not here when we passed earlier. What is that lovely- smelling food cooking in the clay jar? I've never smelled or seen such food as this."

Yeshua smiled. "My Father Yahweh sent angels to

care for My and your needs. Let us first thank Him for His provision. Sit, dear sisters."

He and the three sisters sat around the cooking fire. Yeshua lifted His hands toward the sky; the sisters also lifted their hands.

Yeshua's voice was like a soothing warm wind. "Father, thank You for today and all that You have provided. Thank You for being with Me always, for we are one. Bless this food and water to our bodies. As we partake of this we also accept Your eternal truth to our bodies and spirits with thankfulness. Your will be done in word and deed in our lives. A'ho."

The sisters together said, "A'ho."

Yeshua served each one some fish and some of the food that was in the clay pot, placing the food in large sea clam shells.

The three sisters could not take their eyes off of Him. His presence and voice were so soothing to them. Rainbow Warrior was first to taste the unknown food. She turned towards her sisters and smiled. Running Brook and Shining Dragon Fly tasted the unknown food. They both giggled and took another bite.

Yeshua smiled, "This dish is a gift from Yahweh as a reminder that I came to you. I will give you the seed of these Three Sisters: corn, beans, and squash.

"Dragon Fly, you shall be the representation of corn." Jesus handed Dragon Fly a bag of corn seeds; she opened the bag and took one seed out. He handed Rainbow Warrior a bag of bean seeds. She opened it and took out one seed. He then handed Running Brook a bag of squash seeds; she also took one seed out.

Yeshua spoke as the women ate and examined the seeds, His voice soothing and authoritative. "Dragon Fly, as you are the oldest and the tallest, like corn you will stand tall. Beans will support and stabilize the corn against blustering winds." His words reminded Dragon Fly how much support she received from her sisters.

Yeshua continued speaking. "The sturdy corn stalks will support the twining beans to climb. Rainbow Warrior, like beans you will supply food needed to support both corn and squash. Running Brook, squash's large leaves will help to keep the weeds down and help maintain moisture in the soil. You will also travel far and bring food both physically and spiritually to others. The three foods, when eaten together, are complete. The name I have given for the Three Sisters is Succotash. This example of how different plants help and nurture each other is what you three sisters must remember and teach the next seven generations. Your differences are needed; they are gifted to you from Yahweh for the good of all. You will always be stronger together."

Yeshua's look was loving and kind, yet there was a

sense of seriousness and that they needed to be alert.

Yeshua spoke again. "Plant these together in a mound, to remind you we first ate them at Potumtuk."

Yeshua's countenance changed. He looked resolved as He stated, "The evil-spirited ones will target their attacks through separation, division, and back-biting. Evil-spirited ones hate all that is good; they hate Yahweh and all that He has created. The evil ones steal, kill, and destroy. They only speak lies.

In Yahweh there is togetherness, unity, faith, hope, and love. Serving one another in love, in this there is only goodness and truth. Let us finish our meal. I must go to Wellomuck and see Gives Well."

Dragon Fly investigated Yeshua's face, which remained loving and steadfast. "His transition fire is burning; his travel to the great mystery has begun."

Yeshua smiled and said, "He is my servant, willing to give all, so all will know who Yahweh, Yeshua, and Holy Spirit are. We are givers of life. We are one."

The four finished their meal in silence. Yeshua rose and said, "Follow me."

Dragon Fly, Rainbow Warrior, and Running Brook each said, "I will follow you."

Yeshua asked, "Do you trust Me?"

The three sisters each said, "I do."

"We shall return to Wellomuck on angels' wings." Yeshua raised His hands and said, "Yahweh, send Your angels to carry us to Wellomuck. Close your eyes and hold hands."

They all held hands in a circle with Yeshua and closed their eyes. Peace enveloped them as they entered another realm where time and space had no measurement.

They heard the voice of Yeshua, which sounded like many waters. "Open your eyes." When they opened their eyes, they were standing outside Dragon Fly's longhouse at Gives Well's transition fire. The people that where paying respect to Gives Well's family at the fire outside Dragon Fly's longhouse appeared to be unaware of the sudden appearance of Yeshua and the three sisters.

Yeshua said, "Walk with me; take me to Gives Well." He took Dragon Fly by the hand, and she led him around the right side of her longhouse where Gives Well's body lay on a stilted bed. Rainbow Warrior and Running Brook followed, along with all the relatives and friends that were at the fire.

The friends and relatives did not know why they followed, only that they were drawn to the man with Rainbow Warrior, Dragon Fly, and Running Brook.

Yeshua spoke directly to the three women, "Do you

believe I am the Son of Yahweh and that I can do all Yahweh is able to do?" Each sister said, "I do."

Yeshua spoke to the people who followed them to where Gives Well lay. "Yahweh has given all an eternal gift, to believe that He is. You may embrace or reject Him. If you have rejected Him and have not made Him first as Rainbow Warrior has spoken to you of, please depart from us." Everyone remained.

Chapter 17:
For His Glory

Yeshua stood in front of the stilted bed where Gives Well lay and lifted His hands. "Yahweh, I am here of Your will. I have given Your precepts naturally and spiritually in the form of Three Sisters, corn, beans, and squash, and teaching that unity pleases You. Your will is unity; there is strength in unity. Yahweh, show us You are Creator of all things, and nothing is impossible with You, and we are one. I do only Your will, as I have seen and heard. Yahweh, show us Your glory." Yeshua raised his right hand toward where Gives Well lay and said in a loud voice, "Gives Well, rise from your sleep." Gives Well made a great gasp, as one may when the awe of creation is revealed. Then Gives Well exhaled, sat up, and raised his hands, saying, "Praise Yahweh."

Yeshua turned to the people that were present. "Help Gives Well to come off this death bed and out of those burial clothes. Let us all eat together in celebration of this miracle Yahweh has done. He is the giver of life."

Everyone present appeared to have been given an assignment. There was excitement and laughter in Wellomuk.

Dragon Fly, Good First, and her father It Thunders helped Gives Well down from the stilted burial bed. They walked on either side of him, taking him inside the longhouse to change from his burial clothes.

Once inside their longhouse, he and Dragon Fly embraced. They leaned in, forehead to forehead, chest to chest; their hearts and minds met in a whirlwind of revelation.

"You agreed to this, husband, to be used to show the others Yahweh's Son Yeshua is as Yahweh and you were not allowed to let me know."

"This is true, my wife." Gives Well looked into Dragon Fly's eyes, waiting for her response. She and It Thunders started to disrobe him; she took his hand, looked into his eyes and said, "You're a good man."

"This is not about me, my bride, this is for the glory of Yahweh, His son Yeshua, and the Holy Spirit. They are one. Now let's prepare me to receive a meal; I'm so hungry,"

It Thunders assisted Gives Well out of his burial clothes and his bride redressed him.

Outside, the younger women were preparing a celebration meal. Some of the women prepared venison, turkey, quail, a variety of fish, quohogs, crab, and lobster. Another group of women prepared fiddleheads, wild carrots, mushrooms, berries, honey, and pine.

Yeshua was in the mist of the elder women. He gave them each bags of corn, bean, and squash seed. He taught them how the seed should be planted together in mounds and how each supported the other. He called the combination Three Sisters. The elder woman listened intently, smiled, and nodded to each other as Yeshua touched each one; He imparted His peace.

Yeshua then went to join the children as they gathered wood to keep the fires going. When the task was completed, Yeshua asked the children to sit in a circle. He stood in the middle of the circle; His movements and soothing voice captured the children's attention. The late afternoon air was cool and there was the aroma of honey and pine. The atmosphere was thick with peace.

The children listened intently as He spoke to them of honor, purpose, being led by the Spirit of Yahweh. He said to do well towards all people, the earth, the animals, the air and water. Much of what He spoke of was mysterious, yet all knew every word was truth.

Yeshua beckoned all the children to come to Him in a great embrace. He touched each one's head and blessed them.

As Rainbow Fern soaked in the atmosphere, Yeshua approached her and smiled.

He touched her head. "You see the end from the beginning in others and pray them to their ends. Rainbow Fern, you do this for Yahweh. This is a selfless act; the desires of your heart will not be withheld." He then took a deep breath and blew into Rainbow Fern's face. She inhaled and smiled as she was given visions of angels to guard over each child. Yeshua looked up stretched out His left arm, "Fire Walker, come." Fire Walker walked to Yeshua; he stretched out his right arm. He and Yeshua grasped right forearms. They looked deeply into each other's eyes as if looking for a treasure. Yeshua spoke. "You know of the cleansing power of fire and water. I now give you the breath that bring these all to life." Yeshua took a deep breath and exhaled on Fire Walker. Fire Walker inhaled; he entered a vision of a whirlwind of fire, water, and air that produced purity of heart and mind.

The last sibling to be blessed was One Who Makes All Laugh. Yeshua touched his head. "Oh, you do understand the first will be last and the last will be first." With a twirl and a jump, One Who Makes All Laugh looked Yeshua in the eye and with a voice that was more mature than expected, he said, "I do."

Yeshua, looking at One Who Makes All Laugh, said, "Teach the others." Then Yeshua blew his breath towards One Who Makes All Laugh's face. He inhaled and exhaled saying, "All for the glory of Yahweh."

Yeshua lifted his hand and said, "Three sticks bound together are not easily broken. Come, Rides on Wind, Tender Bear, Screeching Bird."

The three came to him holding hands. Yeshua took hold of Rides on Wind and Screeching Bird's hands, with Tender Bear between them. The three felt a surge of power and peace come from Yeshua to them. "The three of you shall travel to the four ends of the earth, North, South, East and West." Yeshua took a breath and exhaled towards the three siblings. "Wherever you go, you will bring the glory of Yahweh. You all will be my hands and feet; your voices will come from the Holy Spirit. Together you will set many captives free."

The three inhaled and said together, "We will for Your glory, Yahweh."

All the children closed their eyes and entered the great mystery where time and space cannot be measured. The angels tended their needs; each soul was vitalized. There was peace in Wellomuck.

Chapter 18: Never Will I Leave You

It Thunders, in a thunderous voice, said, "Come all, our celebration meal is prepared for the return of Gives Well to us. We have never seen this, but we know that Yahweh has blessed us with His Son Yeshua today, to show us there is nothing impossible with Him. He has shown Himself in bodily form to us through His Son Yeshua. We celebrate His presence here as the giver of life. We give You honor, Yahweh, Yeshua, and Great Spirit and acknowledge You as one. We thank You for Your love and kindness."

It Thunders looked to Yeshua. Yeshua lifted His hands and said," A'ho, I agree. Yahweh, My Father, be pleased with our praise. Bless You for providing us with this food and all we will ever need. We eat with thanksgiving to You."

The entire community thought the food had never tasted so good, water never so refreshing. Everything seemed to be bursting with new life and brilliance. The conversations were life giving, and everyone had moments alone with Yeshua. His words and touch imparted a special gift unique to each person. Every person thought there had never been a greater celebration amongst the Pokanoket Tribe. No one wanted this celebration to end.

When Yeshua spoke all listened; there was complete silence. Peace was tangible; no child or baby fussed in any way. A sign of Yahweh's presence is peace.

"My friends, I must return from where I came. I am pleased to be here now and will one day return, but I will not leave you alone. All who are believers and are willing receive a fresh and deeper impartation of the Great Spirit, the Holy Spirit, come forth."

It appeared that the whole community came forth. Yeshua took a deep breath and exhaled, and a wave of greater love and peace was imparted to everyone. Many were given eyes that were able to see past the ordinary to the extraordinary.

Chapter 18: Never Will I Leave You

Chapter 19:

And This Will be a Sign

Yeshua walked over to Rainbow Warrior. She was sitting with her husband, daughters, their husbands, and her grandchildren. Rainbow Fern was playing with her mother's hair, the boys were arm wrestling. Fire Walker allowed One Who Makes All Laugh win several times before he took a victory. Fire Walker knew how to make his younger brother know his importance to everyone. Sometimes this included allowing him to win and sometimes teaching him how to lose with humility and grace.

Good First sat behind Rainbow Warrior, his arms draped over her shoulders. Both were content to watch their family showing love for each other. Their daughters and husbands snuggled in each other's arms, enjoying food, family, and peace.

Yeshua approached them, smiling. "Beautiful family." Good First answered, "Katabotash (thank you)."

Yeshua said, "Good First, may I have your wife walk with me to my canoe? It is time for my return to where I have come from. I am going to ask her sisters also to come; she will not be left to walk home alone." Good First answered without hesitation, "I trust you, Yeshua."

Rainbow Warrior turned toward her husband. Forehead to forehead they expressed their love toward each other. Good First stood up then assisted Rainbow Warrior up off the ground. "I will get our family home and assist our grandchildren in their prayers. I will lie awake until you return, my bride, Kawannamush," Good First said while lightly touching Rainbow Warrior's shoulder.

"Kawannamush, husband." Rainbow Warrior remembered the first time those words were exchanged between them. In silent prayer she gave thanks to Yahweh for the gift of her husband. He then extended his right arm toward Yeshua; Yeshua did the same. They grasped right forearms, looked directly into each other's eyes, and nodded.

The children stopped what they were doing, ran up to Yeshua, and wrapped their arms around Him.

"Do you really have to leave now?" One Who Makes

All laugh asked.

"I do, but my Great Spirit will stay here with all who call upon Yahweh." Yeshua gently removed His right arm from Good First's right forearm and placed His right hand over One Who Makes All Laugh's heart. "And I would like you, One Who Makes All Laugh, to let others know that for me."

"I will," One who Makes All Laugh said in a strong, convincing voice.

"I know you will," Yeshua said with a smile.

"Your sisters await our joining them, Rainbow Warrior," Yeshua said as He took Rainbow Warriors hand. They met with Dragon Fly and Running Brook. Once the three sisters were together they looked toward all the people of the Pokanoket Tribe. All eyes and ears were upon them. Yeshua smiled and said, "My peace I leave you." All entered His peace.

Yeshua and the three sisters turned and walked together to the path that lead to Potumtuk. They walked in silence, the sisters pondering all that had happened.

The daylight was nearing its end; the sun began to reach the horizon. The color of the sky transitioned from light blue to fiery red, yellow, and orange. When the sun dropped behind the horizon the color of the sky turned to deep blues and purples. The stars began to reveal their presence. The sisters followed where Yeshua led; His footsteps were illuminated with light. The sisters all thought, *I will always follow where Yeshua leads.*

Yeshua, knowing their thoughts, looked back over His right shoulder at the sisters. His eyes were soft, His smile warm, His voice glided over the warm night air. "I know you will always follow where I lead you. I am even now teaching you how to be set apart for my purpose. When tides are out you will have an altar, a visual to remember that I will provide all you need. A physical altar will remind you that I am with you and will provide for your physical, spiritual, and emotional needs. This you must know even when you can't see, touch, or feel it. You will be able to see beyond your body, spirit, and heart. I am always with you. If you are troubled, know I am a very present help in times of trouble. My dear ones, do not fear but be courageous, be very courageous. You have seen with Yahweh death has no sting."

Yeshua's words wooed the women along the path as His steps lit the way. The sisters did not realize until His last word that he had led them not only to Potumtuk but also down the declining path to the ocean edge.

The moon was full and bright, with a red hue to it. The light of the red moon danced on the ocean, the tide low.

The sisters, very focused on Yeshua, did not notice the three large stones shaped as the seeds of corn, bean and squash about 50 feet out from the shoreline.

Yeshua spoke, and His voice sounded as thunder, wind, and many waters, "Behold your altar of remembrance. Remember Yahweh first. Remember Yahweh, I, and the Great Holy Spirit are one. Remember we are always with you even when you do not see or feel us. Never will we leave you; never will we forsake you. Remember that we will provide all you ever need. Remember no storm in your lives will remove us from you. We will never leave or forsake you. We will fight your every battle and we will always be victorious. Remember storms will come, but we are your stability; we cannot be moved. Remember even death does not have rule over Our will for you. Remember we prepare a place for you; this is a great mystery, but we have given you a portion of faith to believe. Remember this; each time the tide goes out these three stones representing our gifts, the Three Sisters, will be seen. Remember all they represent, remember, and tell the next seven generations. Remember even when the waters get high and the stones are not seen they are still there as we and all our provision are for you."

When Yeshua faced the sisters there was fire in His eyes, the eternal fire that never stops burning. He took a breath, exhaled, and blew towards the sisters. "My peace

I leave you."

The sisters together entered the realm where time and space do not exist. They met with family members that had transitioned to the great mystery. They were given gifts for future faith, hope, and love. The greatest gift was love.

Suddenly they were back on the beach; the tide had come in. Yeshua stood in front of them smiling. He opened His arms; the sisters entered His embrace.

Chapter 20:
I Will Return

The embrace the sisters received from Yeshua made them feel complete, whole, full of truth and strength. Yeshua took a small step back. Still smiling He said, "My mission here is finished. I have a people you know not of. I must go to them, for I have a mission that must be finished there. All things are working together for the good of those that love Yahweh. The first will be last and the last will be first. I will return, and when I do, I will be seen by all people; I will ride into this realm on the clouds." He turned towards the ocean where His canoe awaited Him. He entered His canoe and raised His right hand, looking back at the sisters. "Aquene, peace be with you. I am sending you home on wings of angels." There was a bright warm light which caused the sisters to feel extreme peace; they closed their eyes.

When each sister opened her eyes, they found

themselves in their own home lying in their own bedding. Each sister said at the same time, as if they were still united, "Thank You, Yahweh; we await the return of Yeshua. We will remember and do all He has told us. We will teach the next seven generations."

There is complete silence in the community center of the Pokanoket Nation as I, the 12th-generation granddaughter of Rainbow Warrior, say, "My name is Kepenum Nepauzshad, Harvest Moon. These are the prophesies we are to teach the next seven generations. We shall do this until Yeshua returns. We will remember and do what He has taught us; He provides our every need. We will not live in fear but know He prepared us for a time like this. He is always with us, fighting our every battle. We are victorious in Him."

As I, Harvest Moon, speak, I notice a relative, a little five-year-old girl with amber hair and tawny skin with gold tones sitting in the front row, whose eyes are fixed on me. Her name is Rainbow After the Summer Rain.

"Will you continue and agree to remember our role in Yahweh's plan? For this concludes the prophecy."

I look toward Rainbow After the Summer Rain; she looks at me with maturity beyond her age and nods. She and the entire community in unity say a jubilant. "A'ho." The community, in unity, raise hands. Each person verbalizes their own praises, thanksgiving, and commitment to follow Yahweh through Yeshua and to be led by the Holy Spirit. Peace fills hearts and minds.

The community slowly starts to disperse; no child fusses or baby cries. The people of the Pokanoket Tribe leave with confidence that they all have purpose in Yahweh's plan.

The elders often call this time "the time of glory to glory." No one ever leaves the same way they came in. We all long for the next glory. Until the next glory, "Kwannamush, Aquene."

EPILOGUE

From the Author: Though this book is written as fiction, much of it is comprised of true stories from the author's childhood. She was told Yeshua walked with them here on Turtle Island, the name indigenous people call the Americas as we know them now. She was told He gave us the Holy Spirit and told of others that would bring the Word. He gave us provision of the Three Sisters and in the provision are parables denoting the nature of our Heavenly Father, Yahweh, Yeshua and the Holy Spirit.

The Bible was translated into the Algonquin language for the praying Indians of the Pokanoket Tribe and other Northeastern Woodland Tribes at the birth of this nation. He is the God of every tribe and every nation. To all who believe in Him, He gave the right to be a child of God.

All about Yahweh is truth. He loves us, provides for us, fights our every battle and is victorious every time. He visited us, and when He left, He left us Holy Spirit to guide us and comfort us. He is one day to return, and all will look up and see Him return from the sky. He has prepared work and a place for those who know Him. His desire is that none be lost. To know Him is to love Him, for Yahweh is love.

If you want to know Him, if you are not sure you will

go to heaven, ask Him to reveal Himself to you. He has died for a fallen world; acknowledge that in yourself. He became victorious over sin and death so all who believe this may have life eternal in heaven with Him. Ask Him to come and sup with you and teach you His ways, to live life in fullness.

To understand this better, read the book of John in the Bible. Ask a friend who you are certain knows, loves, and follows Jesus. They are the peculiar ones. They love instead of hate, forgive what others call unforgiveable, and believe and see the impossible happen in their lives.

Meanwhile, I am praying for you. Prayer reaches the place where time and space is unmeasurable. Aquene (peace be with you.) Let peace guide you, kwannamush (I love you).

About the Author

Darlene Bruce Spencer is an active member of the Pokanoket Tribe. She sits on the Pokanoket tribal council and is Wolf Clan Mother. She gave her life to the Lord nearly forty years ago, putting her hand to the plow and never looking back.

Darlene has an evangelistic heart sharing the gospel wherever she goes. She is the mother to two wonderful daughters, Jolleen Webster and Jessica Hunt. They are married to the best sons-in-law possible, Fred Webster and Ehrin Hunt.

She has one granddaughter, Ani Webster, and two grandsons, Quinn and Christian Hunt. Darlene is a Christian singer and songwriter. She sings on the worship team at her church and sings with the Pokanoket drum.

She was led by Yeshua to become a registered nurse. She worked as a community nurse for thirty-one years, where she was affectionately referred to as the "singing nurse."

In March of 2021 Darlene heard the Holy Spirt tell her to buy a keyboard. Though not knowing how to play a keyboard, she bought one out of obedience. Before long she was playing the keyboard and writing songs.

Years prior, she was prophesied over, saying she would write a book. Darlene never desired to write a book, but the prophecy lingered in her mind.

An accident occurred at work in September 2021, causing post traumatic concussion syndrome and whiplash. The Lord continued to call her to write a book and to produce a CD. He kept bringing her back to childhood stories told and the statement, "We must teach the next seven generations."

The post traumatic concussion syndrome affected executive functioning, reading, and retrieving words. Neck and shoulder pain, headaches, and lack of sleep were battled daily. Regardless, she continued playing the keyboard, writing songs, and singing, which helped with word retrieval and speech. But she avoided writing. Darlene had discovered that she could not comprehend what she read; prior to the accident she was an avid reader. Now she could not read and comprehend a simple book read to her grandchildren.

She heard the Holy Spirit say, "Do you trust me? Sit down and write for the next seven generations. I will help you."

She did just that, answering, "Yes, I trust you." She sat down and started to write, mostly at night when she couldn't sleep. When she went back and read her writing she was amazed she could comprehend it and often did not remember writing what was written. She gives all glory to the Holy Spirit.

Darlene is still struggling with post traumatic concussion syndrome and pain, but she is doing it with good cheer. Every step of the way, Papa God has provided her every need and is a light to her path. She is currently being led on producing a CD.

Darlene's prayer is that the next seven generations pass on the legacy of Yahweh, Yeshua, and Great Spirit's visitation. He visited yesterday, today, and He is our hope for tomorrow.

CPSIA information can be obtained
at www.ICGtesting.com
Printed in the USA
BVHW051434200723
667552BV00001B/2

9 798890 411846